DEMYSTIFYING CONSULTING SERVICES

THE ULTIMATE GUIDE TO BUILDING STRONG CLIENT RELATIONSHIPS

Ahmed Zouhair

Austin, Texas

Copyright © 2024 by Ahmed Zouhair

The content contained within this book may not be reproduced, duplicated, or transmitted without direct written permission from the author or the publisher.

Legal Notice:
This book is copyright protected. It is only for personal use. You cannot amend, distribute, sell, use, quote or paraphrase any part, or the content within this book, without the consent of the author or publisher.

Demystifying Consulting Services – The Ultimate Guide to Building Strong Client Relationships / Ahmed Zouhair. -- 1st ed.

This book is dedicated to all dedicated consultants, independent consultants, independent contractors, freelancers, small business owners, startups, and entrepreneurs. These people know what it's like to deal with the "good struggle" and understand how to work with fewer resources and get the job done no matter what.

CONTENTS

INTRODUCTION 3
PART 1: DISCOVERY 5
   CHAPTER 1: THE WORLD OF CONSULTING 7
   CHAPTER 2: LAUNCHING YOUR CONSULTING SERVICES 11
PART 2: STRATEGY 21
   CHAPTER 3: NAVIGATING CONSULTING SECTORS 23
   CHAPTER 4: CLIENT RELATIONSHIPS 27
   CHAPTER 5: DELIVERING VALUE 29
   CHAPTER 6: NICHE CONSULTING 33
   CHAPTER 7: DISTINGUISHING YOURSELF IN A CROWDED MARKETPLACE 37
   CHAPTER 8: OVERCOMING CHALLENGES 41
PART 3: PRACTICAL APPLICATION 45
   CHAPTER 9: PERFORMANCE, PLATFORMS, AND PEOPLE 47
   CHAPTER 10: REAL-WORLD EXAMPLES 51
   CHAPTER 11: FINAL THOUGHTS 75
ACKNOWLEDGMENTS 77
ABOUT THE AUTHOR 79

INTRODUCTION

This book serves as a guide to help navigate the complexities of the consulting industry, offering essential insights and strategies for success in this rapidly evolving field. In an era dominated by digital transformation and AI advancements, understanding the nuances of consulting is more critical than ever.

Why Now?

The consulting industry is currently a trillion-dollar business, with forecasts predicting exponential growth in the coming decades. Surveys suggest that a significant portion of the future workforce will be comprised of freelancers, independent consultants, and remote workers. Moreover, projections from the 2024 International Monetary Fund (IMF) report indicate a substantial impact of AI on job markets, potentially saving significant work time and contributing trillions to the global economy.

Why This Book?

Amidst these shifts, the demand for management consulting services continues to surge, driven by robust economic developments across global markets.

This book, this guide, is structured into three key phases: *Discovery*, *Strategy*, and *Application*:

In the *Discovery* phase, we delve into the fundamental aspects of consulting, from its definition to its impacts and the essential skills required for success. We explore launching consulting services and aligning strategically with customer needs. Additionally, we introduce practical frameworks such as the Double Diamond model and Business Model Canvas to aid effective problem-solving.

The *Strategy* phase focuses on cultivating client relationships and niche specialization, while the *Application* phase emphasizes performance measurement (OKRs) and leveraging technology tools and templates.

Lastly, case studies shared by seasoned consultants and independent contractors provide invaluable insights into the paths to becoming a successful consultant, along with the associated challenges. These real-life experiences serve not only to illustrate the value consultants offer but also as inspiration for readers embarking on their consulting journey.

A Little About Me and Why I Wrote This Book

Consultants, at heart, are entrepreneurs (which we'll discuss later in this book).

My entrepreneurial journey began at the young age of fourteen, living in Morocco, spurred by the silent influence of familial role models, including my grandfather and father. With determination as my guiding force, I embarked on a mission to sell Moroccan cookies, navigating the bustling markets of Daoudiate to Jamaa Lafna, known as Malah, on foot. This endeavor, though challenging, instilled in me invaluable lessons in resourcefulness and initiative as I procured sought-after *Coco* and *Palive* cookies and meticulously presented them to neighbors, marking the beginning of my entrepreneurial journey.

My professional journey took me to the United States as a young man, where I found myself in the wrong field—pursuing a degree in petroleum engineering at The University of Texas at Austin. In my heart, I was still an entrepreneur. Eventually, I found my way to becoming a project management professional (PMP) and also earned a doctorate in business administration, building a thriving career and consultancy from scratch.

By writing *Demystifying Consulting Services*, I wanted to share with you the essential ingredients necessary to unlock the business of consulting, drawing upon my own experiences as well as insights gained from seasoned experts, coaches, and mentors whose collective wisdom spans decades.

Let's Go

Are you ready to apply these insights and skills to tackle real-world challenges in the consulting business? Let's embark on this transformative journey together.

PART I

DISCOVERY

CHAPTER 1

THE WORLD OF CONSULTING

What is Consulting?

According to *Webster's Dictionary*, consulting is simply providing professional services or expert advice and recommendations to clients. When discussing consulting services in this book, we refer to Management Consulting which involves offering business guidance on a range of topics such as Technology, AI, Healthcare, Finances, Accounting, Marketing, IT, Telecommunications, Politics, and much more. The main goal here is to help the customer achieve desired outcomes using the knowledge and expertise of consultants.

In general, most consulting gigs are project-based, which means they are temporary, and their scope, timeline, budget, resources, and contract can range from small to large and from private to government-based.

Consulting can be both an art and a science. An art where it can use people's creative skills and a science where it can apply technology to solve customers' issues as seen in the following example:

My project as a consultant with the city of Salt Flats, California. The project was about offering a service to implement a new system with a third partner contractor using a specific software called Cityworks. Here are the details of the consulting job:

The City of Salt Flats felt they needed a system that would help inventory and track their public assets. Most of the city's departments relied heavily on a manual process, which mainly relied on staff memory, outdated spreadsheets and checklists, and a few other imprecise and inefficient systems. The lack of a system to handle all of this led to a random patchwork of processes and procedures that tracked, inspected, and maintained their assets.

The ability to *better* track and *create* a documented historical depiction of asset performance would ensure that the city's staff remained productive and efficient both in the field and at the office. The system also provided significant enhancements to increase oversight and informational management for the leadership team to analyze trends across all city assets.

Thus, as a consultant, my job was to help with the implementation of Cityworks GIS Centric using third-party services to integrate the new system into the city of Salt Flats in Monterey, California, for their parks, facilities, and properties (including the city airport).

IMPACTS OF CONSULTING

- **Smart(er) Choices**: Business leaders consult industry experts when considering major strategy changes. This helps them understand risks and benefits, enabling informed decisions aligned with long-term goals.
- **Problem Resolution**: Consultants offer solutions in the form of expert advice with recommendations for their concerns. The consultants assess the problems, provide sensible recommendations, and assist the company in putting the improvements into practice. The result is a more streamlined and effective operating framework.
- **Improved Performance** and growth of the organization. Consultants help organizations increase their throughput in their supply chain to improve their operational performance overall, lower expenses, and increase their efficiency.

ALIGNMENT

Steve Jobs said that you have to start with the customer experience and work backward to the technology. Where can we take the customer? What are the incredible benefits being offered? You can't start with the technology and try to figure out where you are going to try to sell it. It didn't work with Apple, Tesla, Amazon, Napster, Moviepass, Zappos, and so forth.

When your people, processes, and tools are all aligned, you will be able to create a faster, better, and more efficient roadmap for your business. A roadmap is a game plan showing where you are and what you want to do in order to create a thriving business for your clients for years to come.

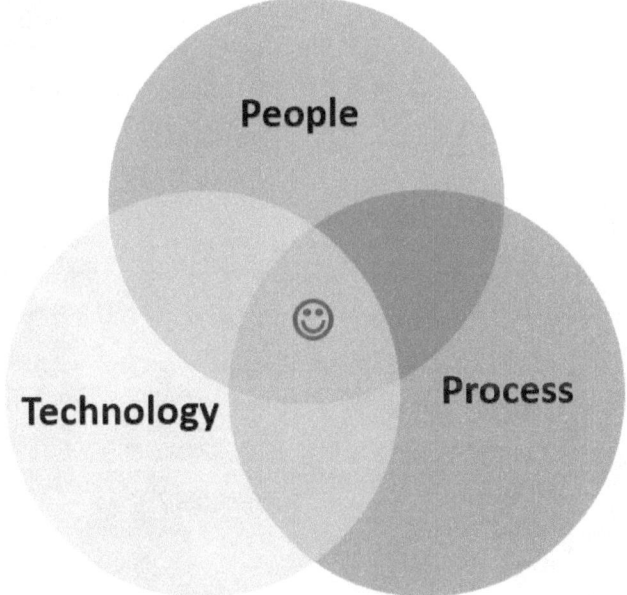

Why start with *People*? People are the backbone of your whole operation. People create strategies for your organization. People build the schedule/plans and not the tools. People will eventually buy your services as well. Thus, technology and processes help facilitate/simplify and streamline our daily operations regarding the *People* we work with and serve.

Once we understand, at the very least, who we serve, we will get closer to being able to launch our consulting services. Let's start at the very beginning... a very good place to start.

CHAPTER 2

LAUNCHING YOUR CONSULTING SERVICES

THE BASICS OF GETTING STARTED

Starting a consulting career may be a fulfilling experience that provides chances for both personal and professional development and the ability to have a significant effect on both individual people and corporations. Whether you're a fresh graduate looking to go into consulting or moving from a new or adjacent field, these tips can help you on your way to building a lucrative consulting career.

- **Self-Reflection and Skill Assessment**: Consider your areas of knowledge, hobbies, and talents. Think about the abilities you have, such as communication, analytical thinking, and problem-solving, that are relevant to consulting positions. Determine any areas where your skill set is lacking, then look for ways to advance your career. This may entail taking seminars, earning certificates, or going to more classes that are related to your consulting specialty.
- **Define Your Consulting Niche**: Choose the precise sector or functional area in which you wish to specialize. Your hobbies and talents should match your specialization. Your knowledge

base grows, and you become a more in-demand consultant in that specific field when you specialize.
- **Build a Strong Educational Foundation**: Keep up with evolving technology, best practices, and industry trends. Ongoing education is crucial in the ever-changing consulting industry. To expand your knowledge base, consider obtaining higher education degrees or certificates in relevant fields.
- **Gain Practical Experience**: In your preferred consulting field, look for freelancing, part-time, volunteering, mentorship, and internship options. Not only can practical experience improve your personal and professional development, but it also offers insightful knowledge about real-world consulting difficulties.
- **Network Strategically**: Participate at major events, meetups, associations, conferences, networking events, and industry events. Establish relationships with experts in the subject of your choice. Use social media sites like LinkedIn to network with business leaders and establish a powerful online presence.

Skills Required and Networking Tips

To succeed in the ever-changing and client-focused world of consulting, one must possess a broad range of fundamental abilities. Among these, effective communication skills is one of the most important. Consultants must be able to communicate difficult concepts to a wide range of audiences both orally and in writing. Strong analytical and problem-solving abilities are equally important because they enable consultants to break down complex problems, provide well-thought-out solutions, and produce measurable outcomes. Furthermore, consultants need to be exceptionally flexible since they have to be able to move across different businesses and quickly adjust to changing project needs. Effective task supervision, achieving deadlines, and guaranteeing project success all depend on having strong project management abilities. Furthermore, developing rapport with customers and encouraging cooperative relationships within teams requires a deep grasp of interpersonal dynamics and emotional intelligence.

Networking is an important part of anyone's career because it is a powerful tool for growth, enabling us to tap into a wealth of resources, knowledge, and support. Understanding the various aspects of networking can empower us to build meaningful connections, navigate business growth and career paths, and achieve our goals. By embracing effective networking techniques and cultivating a supportive network, we can unlock our true potential and create a pathway to success in all facets of life.

Aspiring consultants should be going to industry conferences, seminars, and networking gatherings to network with seasoned experts and learn about current trends in the business. By using internet resources, in particular LinkedIn, consultants can establish a powerful online presence, highlight their areas of expertise, and establish connections with prospective customers or partners

Attending informative interviews and looking for mentorship opportunities expands one's network by offering insightful advice and cultivating connections with people who have experienced the consulting world. To put it simply, having a strong network and well-honed expertise(s) sets consultants up for success in a competitive and dynamic market.

THE "C'S" OF CONSULTING

The core of being a great consultant is not just about being well-read or an expert in your chosen field. The most effective consultant requires a *Can*-do mindset, along with several other "C's".

Consistency

Consistency isn't a "nice to have" but a requirement because we all have to show up every day for work (and for life) regardless of most circumstances, rain or shine, or else there will be undesirable consequences. Consistency is also ingrained into our humanity—

humans have a desire to be consistent in their words and actions. How can and how will you showcase your ability to be consistent?

Curiosity

Be interested in people rather than trying to be interesting. People take an interest in people who are interested in them. We employ this via active listening and asking the right questions. Smiling can help build rapport in many cultures and generate positive reactions and responsiveness.

According to psychologist Paul Ackerman, we activate the autonomic nervous system when we smile, which releases endorphins in the body and makes us feel comfortable. At the same time, we seem to become likable to other people. Handshakes, especially when meeting someone for the first time (depending on one's culture), should always be offered with eye contact and a warm smile.

Building rapport is crucial to showing curiosity about another person, but it's difficult to do when you're nervous. When a person is nervous, they speak faster. Try to do the opposite by slowing down and pausing so the other person feels more at ease, which will lead them to want to engage with you.

Clarity

Clarity helps in the achievement of goals, providing individuals and companies with a clear understanding of their objectives, purpose, and desired out-comes. Clarity assists people and companies in identifying priorities, making effective decisions, and staying committed to objectives. Clarity helps clear mental clutter, such as distractions, negative self-talk, and self-doubt (which can come up when trying to build and foster new relationships).

Clarity is simplicity that gets rid of complexity and is the best friend of priorities. If you lack clarity, nothing will be done right, and like my grandma used to joke and say, "It'll be as clear as mud".

Concentration

We get bombarded by so many "priorities" from both personal and professional parts of life in so many forms (phone calls, texts, emails, in person, and so forth). We have to pick one or else we will be stuck in place.

Research suggests that focus can be trained and improved through various techniques. Mindfulness, which can be as simple as observing your breath, for instance, has been shown to enhance attentional control and reduce mind-wandering. Cognitive training programs that target working memory and executive functions have also demonstrated improvements in concentration. For instance, individuals who regularly practice mindfulness may experience improved focus and attention in their daily lives, allowing them to better concentrate on tasks.

Of course, when consulting and engaging in conversation with clients, concentrating and giving the other person your full attention truly helps in building rapport.

Understanding the Consulting Landscape

To start, make sure you understand the lingo and jargon of the niche in which you'll be consulting and the language your customer speaks. If you don't have a thorough understanding of even basic vocabulary, you won't be able to collaborate and communicate effectively with colleagues in your in space or potential clients.

You must do thorough research on all aspects of your chosen sector. It's also good to have a broad range of knowledge across different kinds of consulting, such as Finance, AI, or Design, mainly so you can see if there are patterns that hold true across sectors (e.g., pricing and pricing tiers, degrees or certificates required, and so on). It's also a good idea to understand what attributes or skill sets make a consultant successful—things like flexibility, problem-solving abilities, and strong people skills are essential.

Clarifying the benchmarks that define a successful consulting firm involves discussing platforms, client rosters, and success metrics. Continuously delivering value, achieving project objectives, and ensuring client satisfaction are integral components of these criteria. A consultant's reputation and level of expertise are evidenced by their performance and adept execution of ongoing projects.

Consulting services typically entail project-based engagements structured around budgets, milestones, deadlines, and resource allocation necessary to fulfill organizational objectives. Project durations can vary significantly, spanning from months to years, contingent upon the nature of the organization and whether contracts are with governmental or non-governmental entities. The consulting process or framework is often tailored to the specific needs of each client. While numerous frameworks exist, it's important not to become overly fixated on any single one, as each client may require customization based on their preferences and requirements.

The Process

Many organizations use different frameworks like Waterfall, Agile, Hybrid, Lean, Six Sigma, and more. My favorite, the Double Diamond framework, is based on Design Thinking.

Additional Frameworks

BRD/CRD

The Business Requirements Document (BRD) or the Customer Requirements Document (CRD) defines the business objectives and the requirements of the customer requesting the service or product.

This document is created by the customers or business representatives and reviewed and approved by the project stakeholders, which can consultants. You can find more information on the BRD / CRD documents online.

Business Model Canvas (BMC)

BMC is a strategic management template that helps businesses to plan their business model simply and clearly. It consists of nine building blocks that represent the different elements of a business model:

BMC Aspect	Description
Definition	A visual tool to plan and explain how a business makes money.
Purpose	Helps design, communicate, improve, and adapt a business strategy.
Building Blocks	**Value Proposition:** What problem do you solve for customers? **Customer Segments:** Who are your ideal customers? **Channels:** How do you reach your customers? **Customer Relationships:** Type of relationship you have with customers. **Revenue Streams:** How do you generate income? **Key Resources:** What assets do you need? **Key Partners:** Who are your critical collaborators? **Key Activities:** What essential actions must you take to deliver value? **Key Capabilities:** What special skills or expertise are required?
Benefits	Flexible, usable by any business size or industry, aids in planning, communication, and presentations.

Several Benefits of Frameworks
- **Structured approach:** Helps guide you through a step-by-step process to fix any business problem, making it easier to tackle.
- **Thorough analysis:** Ensures all important details are considered and addressed.
- **Faster solutions:** Uses proven methods to save time and avoid dead ends to get quick(er) outcomes.
- **Saves Time:** A framework already has a basic structure (blueprint) in place, meaning you don't need to waste time building a new one from scratch. You're able to devote time to solving real problems that matter.
- **Strong Foundation:** A good framework ensures a solid structure, just like a strong foundation keeps a house from falling apart.
- **Easy Customization:** While a framework provides the basics, you can still customize it.

BUSINESS PLAN

A business plan is a document that serves as a roadmap guiding the launch and or growth of a new business. It is a template that includes instructions for each section of the business plan, followed by corresponding fillable worksheet/s (See SCORE.org for more information about the business plan).

NEXT STEPS

Now that we have a better understanding of the basics, it's time to move onto the next phase of your journey as a successful consultant—strategy.

DEMYSTIFYING CONSULTING SERVICES... • 19

PART 2

STRATEGY

CHAPTER 3

NAVIGATING CONSULTING SECTORS

Consultants must have a deep awareness of the different industries and markets they wish to serve. Consultants serve a wide range of industries in both private and public sectors (for-profits and non-profits), including Business, Management, Strategy, Information Technology, Telecommunication, Energy, Construction, Artificial Intelligence, Energy, Services, Automotive, Healthcare, Finance, Human Resources, and more.

Every industry has its own unique challenges, difficulties, and dynamics that call for certain skills and knowledge. For example, Project Management consultants are responsible for managing all kinds of projects, and to do so, they need soft skills like leadership, communication, collaboration, and negotiation. A strategy consulting assignment may entail assisting a business with tasks like navigating market upheaval, removing a huge risk, saving the company forum going under, aligning and streamlining processes with their business goals, and/or identifying growth potential. A consultant in the technology industry may help implement new ideas, digital changes, or cybersecurity plans into practice. Healthcare consultants can assist with enhancing patient care, streamlining procedures, and guaranteeing adherence to industry rules. By researching the broad field of consulting and engaging with colleagues, you can benefit from the industry's culture of knowledge-sharing, gaining new insights and learning best practices in a variety of industries. See table below:

Items	Source Name/Description
Consulting Forums	Consultant Journal Forum, CaseInterview Forum, Wall Street Oasis, Reddit, Top Consultant, ConsultingBuzz Forum, MBA Crystal Ball, Management Consulting Forum
Consulting Firm Websites	McKinsey & Company - Bain & Company - Boston Consulting Group (BCG) - Deloitte - PwC - EY
Professional Associations	Institute of Management Consultants (IMC) - Association of Management Consulting Firms (AMCF)
Industry Reports, White Papers, Books	*The McKinsey Way* by Ethan M. Rasiel, *The Consulting Bible* by Alan Weiss, others written by experienced consultants
Online Courses and Platforms	Coursera, LinkedIn Learning, Udemy (Courses on consulting skills, frameworks, and industry-specific knowledge)
Open AI's Consulting Playbook	Explore OpenAI's interactive guide for an overview of the consulting process using GPT-3
Additional Sources	Blogs, Podcasts, YouTube, Websites; Consultant-Industry-Specific Publications: TED Talks on Business (ted.com); Industry Conferences; Social Media Groups; Industry Events; Business Publications - *Harvard Business Review* (HBR) - *Forbes* - *The Economist* - *Financial Times*

CHAPTER 4

CLIENT RELATIONSHIPS

Apart from proficient communication, negotiations, and leadership, several other strategies may be. Trust is foundational and is simply based on honesty, integrity, and commitment. The consultant's credibility and the client's confidence are strengthened when they consistently produce actual value and exceed the client's expectations. Bottom line—getting the job done is key to a great long-term relationship.

Good client relationship management goes beyond dealing with clients on a project basis. Establishing a personal connection, learning about the client's business objectives, and recognizing significant accomplishments within the company all help to create a more lasting and meaningful collaboration. Furthermore, using customer survey is essential for ongoing development. Customers like consultants who actively solicit feedback, pay attention to their issues, and apply what they've learned to their methods because it shows that they are dedicated to continuous improvement and excellence.

Furthermore, effective customer interactions involve proactive problem-solving. A proactive and client-centric strategy means anticipating problems, providing solutions before they become more serious, and showing dedication to the client's success. Adaptability and flexibility are also critical qualities; the consultant's capacity to change course in response to evolving client demands or project specifications demonstrates their adaptability and commitment to client satisfaction.

CHAPTER 5

DELIVERING VALUE

A successful consulting engagement involves delivering business value, which calls on consultants to prioritize observable and quantifiable results that directly support the client's goals and objectives. Beyond simply making suggestions, tangible value is putting solutions into practice that provide quantifiable gains in terms of more sales, better operational efficiency, higher customer happiness, and/or exceeding OKRs and or KPIs. Consultants must align their actions with the strategic goals of their clients, making sure that they are providing the expected and desired outcomes for their clients.

The most effective way to demonstrate how one can provide concrete value is via compelling case studies, which we will provide In Chapter 10. These case studies are practical illustrations of the consultant's capacity to recognize problems and challenges, create winning plans of action, and produce tangible outcomes. A case study on management consulting, for example, may describe how a consultant improved organizational procedures, which resulted in a large decrease in operating expenses and an increase in total productivity. A case study in technology consulting might describe how a digital transformation plan was successfully implemented, leading to better systems, improved user experiences, and more productivity. Several of the case studies provided will also help you understand the paths to becoming a consultant and the challenges associated.

No matter what path or industry you choose as a consultant, once the client finds value in your services, they will make sure to retain your services and perhaps even share the value you provide with others whom you may call "client" in the future.

CHAPTER 6

NICHE CONSULTING

Specializing in a certain sector, role, or range of services and providing distinctive and specific knowledge and focused solutions to a specific market niche is known as niche consulting. The opportunity to become recognized as an authority in a particular field is one of the key advantages of niche consulting. By focusing more narrowly and developing in-depth knowledge in a particular field, consultants may set themselves apart from generalists and draw in customers looking for specialized insights and solutions. Due to their perceived deep awareness of their unique difficulties and needs, customers view niche consultants as having greater credibility and trust as a result of their specialty.

The possibility of increased income is an additional benefit of niche consulting. Consultants that possess specialized knowledge can charge higher fees for their services. When dealing with complicated or industry-specific challenges, clients are frequently prepared to pay more for consultants who possess specialized expertise and experience. Moreover, niche consulting may result in special classified innovative projects for the government that require a long-term engagement and commitment. Consultants can more easily interact with potential customers who are especially looking for knowledge in their particular field by customizing their messaging and marketing to a focused audience.

First and foremost, in order to pinpoint prospective niches with unmet requirements or underdeveloped consumers, one must do comprehensive market research. Consultants can better adapt their services to satisfy unique requests by having an understanding of the potential and problems within a specialized market. Building a strong network within the selected specialty is just as crucial. A consultant can increase their exposure and credibility by establishing connections with influential people in the field, keeping up with current developments, and actively taking part in communities or events pertaining to their specialization.

Networking is an important part of anyone's career because it is a powerful tool for growth, enabling us to tap into a wealth of resources, knowledge, and support. Understanding the various aspects of networking can empower us to build meaningful connections, navigate business growth and career paths, and achieve our goals. By embracing effective networking techniques and cultivating a supportive network, we can unlock our true potential and create a pathway to success in all facets of life.

Additionally, in the field of niche consulting, ongoing learning and certifications are required and essential to your success. Keeping up with changes in the industry, new technology, and the development of new best practices guarantees that consultants will always have an advantage over the competition and be able to provide their customers with creative solutions. Lastly, in the field of specialist consulting, listening, communication, negotiation, and public speaking skills are all necessary skills. Consultants should explain the distinct value they offer to small or large audiences and show how their specialist knowledge solves certain problems within the industry.

CHAPTER 7

DISTINGUISHING YOURSELF WITHIN THE MARKETPLACE

Marketing

Building a successful career requires effective self-marketing, particularly in the competitive and dynamic consulting industry. In order to draw in prospects, clients, and partnerships, the process entails exhibiting one's abilities, knowledge, and distinctive value offer. Developing a solid online presence is essential to self-marketing success. Professionals need to have an online presence on digital platforms such as social media and personal websites. They should also be speaking at major conferences and writing books and articles/papers for major publications (*Harvard Business Review, Forbes,* etc.) to share their knowledge and views, highlight their successes, and interact with their tribe.

Branding

Branding is simply building a great name for yourself and creating a professional identity that showcases your distinctive value proposition disseminated on a consistent basis across a range of media. Personal branding is having a unique and special competency in your line of business. Professionals may develop credibility and trust, which are important components in drawing customers and prospects, by continuously showcasing a consistent and appealing personal and professional brand. Bottom line—branding is building a strong reputation with your clients, enough so that they have no problem saying nice things about you when you are not around.

Thought Leadership

Professionals establish themselves as an authority in their sector by giving insightful opinions on their specialized knowledge along with industry insights. Writing books and or papers, making contributions to trade journals, offering workshops, and giving presentations at webinars and major conferences may all help achieve this.

Networking

Professionals may network with colleagues, possible clients, and partners by actively participating in industry events, conferences, and online forums. Making a good and lasting impression involves having meaningful discussions, volunteering and mentoring, and adding value to those in your professional network.

CHAPTER 8

OVERCOMING CHALLENGES

Any career path involves overcoming challenges, but in the consulting industry, where complexity and unpredictability are commonplace, resilience and adaptation are essential. Managing client expectations is a regular problem for consultants. It can be challenging to match expectations with what is practically attainable. The key to addressing this is healthy and effective communication. It is easier to manage and align client expectations when project scope, deliverables, and dates are clearly defined early on, and open lines of communication are maintained throughout the engagement. Frequent check-ins and progress reports help guarantee that clients are informed of the progress of their projects at hand.

Handling a client organization's opposition to change is another common difficulty in consulting. You may have heard this statement before: "This is how we have always been doing things. We are not going to change." Clients who may be used to current methods may oppose the implementation of new processes or procedures. Consultants must need buy-ins from their clients by, for example, including leaders and managers in important decision-making, involving stakeholders early in the process, and effectively articulating the advantages of the suggested changes. Creating a coalition of allies within the company who understand and support the suggested modifications may greatly reduce opposition and help projects run smoothly, ensuring the consulting job is executed and implemented successfully.

Furthermore, resource limitations frequently provide difficulties for consulting tasks. Progress might be hampered by poor requirements, limited budget, tight schedule, and lack of resources. To avoid such issues, consultants should proactively identify possible resource restrictions, inform customers of these limitations, and collaborate to discover innovative solutions. This might entail rearranging the order of importance of activities, looking for different data sources, or suggesting phased project techniques that make use of the resources at hand.

PART 3

PRACTICAL APPLICATION

CHAPTER 9

PERFORMANCE, PLATFORMS, AND PEOPLE

Performance

One must define objectives and measure outcomes to encourage better performance. The OKR methodology can help with that and was created by Andy Grove at Intel. It is used by companies such as Google, Intel, Airbnb, and Facebook, as well as Bono of U2 fame and Bill Gates of the Bill and Melinda Gates Foundation, among others. Anyone can use the OKR methodology; especially folks seeking to transition into the role of consultant.

So...what are OKRs?

At its essence, the OKR methodology is a tool often used in project management to achieve a goal measurably and transparently.

The "O" or "Objective" should describe a desired goal or outcome. It is "what" you want to achieve. Note that any goal or outcome should be SMART or Specific, Measurable, Attainable, Realistic, and Time-bound. An example of an objective may be, "By March 21st of this year, I want to be hired in a VP of Sales position for the Fortune 500 company Performance Automotive."

The "KR" is for "Key Results" and is the part where you benchmark, monitor, and measure your progress on the way to achieving your objective. When setting your Key Results, again, they should follow the

SMART acronym. You either meet the requirements or you don't; it's that simple. For example: "By January 3rd, I want to have set up informational interviews with three members of Performance Automotive's sales team. To do this, I will scour my network for contacts, and I will reach out on LinkedIn as well."

The OKR methodology is a tool that can be used to measure progress and to help you stay on track with your goal. OKRs create a sense of clarity and satisfaction and help you perform at a high level, aligning every aspect and element of achieving your end goal from top to bottom.

One of the most satisfying feelings during consulting, of which the OKR process is a part, is completion or satisfying the end goal. A postmortem session (you can do this solo, with a mentor, and/or a mastermind group), is a time for reflection on lessons learned while on the journey toward your end goal, in this case, the consulting job you've been hired to undertake in order to meet your client's needs.

Some questions to ask yourself during your postmortem session could be:

1. Did my OKRs meet my requirements?
2. What went right?
3. What went wrong?
4. What will I do differently next time?

Example:

Objective: I want to get hired as an independent consultant for the company PMTC.

KR1: Determine the requirements needed to be a consultant for PMTC company.

KR2: Gain personal and professional development needed to get hired as a consultant for PMTC.

KR3: Set a date/time to get started.

KR4: Determine the resources needed to be a consultant for PMTC company.

Platforms

Here are some examples of platforms that can be used to help you narrow down how and where you want to get started in your consulting career.

Category	Consulting Firms
Management Consulting	McKinsey & Company, Boston Consulting Group (BCG), Bain & Company
Professional Services	Deloitte, PwC (PricewaterhouseCoopers), KPMG, EY (Ernst & Young)
Technology Consulting	Accenture, Capgemini, Cognizant, Hitachi Consulting
Strategy Consulting	Oliver Wyman, Roland Berger, A.T. Kearney, LEK Consulting
Financial Consulting	Grant Thornton, Alvarez & Marsal, Protiviti, FTI Consulting
Diversified Consulting	BearingPoint, Navigant Consulting (Guidehouse), IHS Markit
Technology and Digital Transformation	Toptal, Business Talent Group (BTG), Accenture, Hitachi Vantara, Cognizant, Capgemini
Financial Advisory and Risk Management	Protiviti, Alvarez & Marsal, Grant Thornton, FTI Consulting
Healthcare Consulting	Navigant Consulting (Guidehouse)

Freelance Platforms	Upwork, Fiverr, Freelancer.com, Guru, Moonlighting
On-Demand Consulting	Catalant, Business Talent Group (BTG), Expert360
Specialized Consulting	CrowdCube (for crowdfunding and consulting), Toptal (specializing in top freelancers), Catalant (focuses on business expertise)

PEOPLE

While processes and tools are crucial for conducting business in consulting services, people are the most critical for the success of any operation. They bring the knowledge, skills, and creativity to execute processes, and they adapt and innovate using available tools. Investing in the personal and professional development of people is an investment in the overall success of any organization.

CHAPTER 10

REAL-WORLD EXAMPLES

The most effective way to demonstrate the idea of consulting providing concrete value is via compelling case studies. These real-world case studies are practical illustrations of the consultant's capacity to recognize problems and challenges, create winning plans of action, and produce tangible outcomes. A case study on management consulting, for example, may describe how a consultant improved organizational procedures, which resulted in a large decrease in operating expenses and an increase in total productivity. A case study in technology consulting might describe how a digital transformation plan was successfully implemented, leading to better systems, better user experiences, and more productivity. Finally, case studies provided by some consultants and independent contractors at the end of this chapter will help you understand the paths to becoming a consultant and the challenges associated with them.

TREVOR PERRY

THE PERSPECTIVE CATALYST, STORYTELLER, AND IN-DEMAND KEYNOTE SPEAKER

Several of my "superiors" at my most recent full-time employer told me I had to change my Facebook profile to represent my employment with them. *Why?* I wondered. *It's my personal page.*

The first time I introduced my strategy methodology to my employer, I was told, "That's not how we do it here," even after they recognized it was an effective approach. Why? I was hired for my skill set.

A recommendation by the team for a customer transformation project was a multi-year program that would not be uncomfortable given their department's annual budget. The "higher-ups" told the team the project needed to be nine times higher in cost and exclusively use our own tools regardless of their mismatch to the effort. Why? Is the customer ignorant enough to hock everything to achieve a much worse ROI?

I was once stirred to write an article for the greater community to warn them of vendor predatory practices. Without naming the vendors, one would think they would recognize their behavior and work to resolve such negative anti-customer tactics. They continue to mislead and misrepresent and sometimes wonder why they are not achieving the results their VCs require.

My personal experiences working for an employer have raised these questions.

Is it better to offer a reasonable project and get the work, or to offer an inflated, unreasonable project that investors like and lose the business?

Is it better to improve the performance of the equipment to allow it to postpone the expense of an upgrade, or to force the upgrade now and lose the customer's faith and, most likely, their business?

Is it better to have a long relationship with a customer based on mutual benefits, or to sell them something they don't need based on a deadline from management, and lose the customer's long-term business?

I struggled mightily in my career as an employee when I put the customer first. Fighting those who had motives that were, generally, not shared with the employees, became draining. At one point, I was censured because I did not do what was not communicated to me.

Sure, you may have the skills for the task, but when you don't know the specifics of the task, you will fail.

Becoming an independent consultant afforded me the opportunity to work with customers to see them succeed without being snowed by a vendor whose investors demand profits. The long-term business relationships that were fostered were rewarding, both ethically and financially.

Looking back, I see that prioritizing customers' needs is an approach that suits my personal morals and ethics. My independence provides me with the right place and space to achieve those.

YASSINE TOUIMI BENJELLOUN

TECHNOLOGY CONSULTING SAP PARTNER AT DEXTON CONSULTING

The transition from the structured world of a multinational firm to the dynamic realm of IT consulting marks a journey filled with aspirations, challenges, and transformative growth. This narrative seeks to offer a comprehensive overview of the IT consulting journey—highlighting the initial motivations, the realities of the profession, the challenges faced, and the lessons learned along the way from my own modest experience. Through this exploration, the aim is to demystify the field of IT consulting, providing insights and inspiration for those considering a similar career path.

Sparking the Change

My professional odyssey began within the secure yet confining boundaries of full-time employment, where the yearning for a more impactful and autonomous role grew increasingly potent. This restlessness catalyzed my leap into consulting, a domain where the potential for innovation and direct client impact promised a fulfilling career. The decision was driven by a desire to harness my expertise in technology more creatively and meaningfully, shaping solutions that resonate on a deeper level with client needs.

Navigating the Consulting Odyssey

The shift to consulting was a dive into uncharted waters, marked by the exhilaration of new challenges and the daunting task of establishing oneself in a competitive field. Among the early trials was a significant client engagement that tested my commitment and resilience, demanding a two-hour commute each way and the adaptability to work on-site without the convenience of remote work. This experience underscored the essence of consulting: the dedication to go beyond expectations while balancing professional demands with personal sacrifices.

Demystifying the Consultant's Role

In the realm of IT consulting, the primary mission is to act as a bridge between the potential of technology and the practical needs of businesses. Consultants assess existing IT infrastructures, identify inefficiencies, and craft strategies that align with business objectives. They are strategists, advisors, and implementers, skilled in translating complex technical concepts into actionable business insights, thereby driving innovation and efficiency.

Confronting Challenges, Embracing Rewards

The journey of a consultant is fraught with challenges, from the unpredictability of project flows to the complexities of managing a consulting business. The unpredictability of the human factor and the demands of internal management reveal the nuanced struggles within the consulting industry. Despite these hurdles, the rewards of consulting are profound. Dexton Consulting, where I played a pivotal role in its inception, exemplifies the potential within this industry. Though not yet at the pinnacle of leadership, its rapid growth and the interest from major firms for partnerships underscore the value and impact of our work.

Lessons from the Frontlines

The pathway to excellence in IT consulting is paved with continuous learning, the art of relationship building, and enduring resilience. Each of these pillars not only defines the consultant's role but also distinguishes the exceptional from the merely competent.

The Lifelong Learner's Quest

In the rapidly shifting sands of technology and business, the consultant's most potent tool is knowledge. Continuous learning transcends the acquisition of new technologies or methodologies; it encompasses a deep understanding of industry trends, business strategies, and the socio-economic factors influencing the tech landscape. This commitment to learning is what allows a consultant to offer solutions that are not just effective today but are resilient and adaptable for the future.

The quest for knowledge is both a personal and professional journey. Personally, it demands a mindset of curiosity and humility—a recognition that no matter the level of expertise attained, there is always more to learn. Professionally, it requires a strategic approach to education, selecting areas of learning that align with both market needs and personal passion. This dual focus ensures that the consultant remains at the forefront of innovation, ready to meet the challenges of tomorrow with insight and agility.

The Art of Relationship Building

The foundation of a successful consulting career is built on the relationships forged along the way. Trust, nurtured over countless interactions, becomes the bedrock of these relationships. It is trust that transforms a consultant from an external advisor into a valued partner. Achieving this level of relationship goes beyond technical excellence; it requires empathy, reliability, and an unwavering commitment to the client's success.

Empathy allows a consultant to truly understand a client's needs and concerns, going beyond the surface level to uncover the root of challenges. Reliability, demonstrated through consistent performance and accountability, builds confidence in the consultant's capabilities and intentions. Together, these qualities create a powerful synergy, fostering collaborations that are both productive and enduring.

The Chronicles of Resilience

The journey into consulting is replete with challenges, each serving as a crucible for growth. An early, vivid example from my career involved a client requiring extensive commuting, a scenario that tested the limits of my perseverance. This engagement was not merely a logistical challenge but a lesson in resilience, teaching me the importance of maintaining focus and motivation in the face of adversity.

Resilience in consulting goes beyond enduring long hours or complex projects; it involves an adaptive mindset that views challenges as opportunities for growth. This mindset, cultivated through experiences like early client engagement, becomes a defining attribute of a successful consultant. It ensures that no matter the difficulty faced, the consultant can navigate through it, learning and emerging stronger on the other side.

These lessons from the frontlines are not just strategies for success but are the very essence of what it means to be a consultant in the IT industry. They embody the consultant's journey, from the initial steps into the profession to the pinnacle of achievement, guiding a path that is both challenging and immensely rewarding.

Reflections

The consulting journey, inherently filled with challenges and opportunities, has paved the way for significant growth, both professionally and for Dexton Consulting. As we stand on the cusp of new beginnings, reflecting on the path traversed offers both a sense of accomplishment and a blueprint for the future. The next steps for us involve two critical phases: stabilizing the business and initiating the offshoring of our services.

Stabilizing the Business

The initial phase of stabilization is crucial. It's about ensuring that Dexton Consulting not only maintains its current trajectory of growth but also builds a robust foundation that can withstand the fluctuations of the market. This involves refining our operational efficiencies, deepening client relationships, and solidifying our position in the market. Achieving stability means moving beyond the startup phase, where every day is about survival, to a phase where strategic planning takes precedence.

Stabilization also means investing in our people and processes. Developing a strong internal culture that embraces our core values of continuous learning, resilience, and relationship building is vital. It's about creating an environment where our team can thrive, fostering innovation, and ensuring that we continue to deliver exceptional value to our clients.

Starting the Offshoring of Our Services

With a stable foundation in place, the next ambitious step involves the offshoring of our services. This strategic expansion is driven by the desire to tap into global talent pools, enhance our service offerings, and reach new markets. Offshoring presents an opportunity to operate around the clock, offering our clients unparalleled support and access to a broader range of services.

The move towards offshoring is not without its challenges. It requires meticulous planning, from selecting the right locations to ensuring cultural and operational alignment. However, the potential rewards are significant. By leveraging global talent, we can enhance our competitiveness, diversify our insights, and offer more innovative solutions to our clients.

Looking Ahead

As Dexton Consulting embarks on these next steps, our commitment to hard work, strategic acumen, and resilience remains unwavering. The path ahead is exciting, offering new avenues for growth and the opportunity to solidify our position in the global consulting landscape.

For those contemplating or embarking on a consulting journey, the roadmap is clear. It's about building a stable foundation, embracing strategic expansion, and always looking for opportunities to innovate and grow. The consulting world offers a unique platform for significant achievements, providing a canvas to paint a career that is as rewarding as it is challenging.

The future of Dexton Consulting and the consulting industry at large is bright and filled with possibilities and opportunities to make a lasting impact. As we move forward, our focus on continuous learning, relationship building, and overcoming challenges will guide us toward new horizons, shaping the future of consulting in an ever-evolving business and technological landscape.

JOSHUA RIVEDAL

KEYNOTE SPEAKER ON RESILIENCE AND MENTAL HEALTH, AUTHOR, FOUNDER/CEO THE I'MPOSSIBLE PROJECT

As the curtains rose on my career, I found myself swept up in the electrifying world of show business. At the tender age of 19, I took my first steps onto the professional stage, fueled by a passion for acting that burned brightly within me. From regional theaters to the bustling streets of New York City, I chased my dreams with dedication and determination.

The bright lights of television and Broadway beckoned, but the path to success was fraught with challenges. Despite my best efforts and working primarily as a voiceover and theater actor, I soon realized that the roles I coveted were few and far between. Faced with fierce competition and the harsh realities of the industry, I knew that I needed to carve out my own path if I wanted to thrive.

And so, I turned to the power of creation. Armed with pen and paper, I began to write, pouring my heart and soul into crafting plays that spoke to me and to the human experience. Gradually, I traded in the uncertainty of auditions for the freedom of artistic expression while producing theater (my own plays and others' as well) that resonated with audiences in ways I never imagined possible.

Yet, even as I pursued my passion on the stage, I found myself grappling with uncertainty and doubt. The sudden departure of my talent manager/agent left me reeling, a setback that threatened to derail my dreams. Not long after that loss, I faced a loss of greater magnitude—the loss of my father to suicide. This tragic and traumatic experience shook me to my core and forced me to confront the fragility of life itself. Over the next 18 months, life for me got darker and darker and simply living and staying alive became a greater challenge with each passing day.

In the midst of darkness, however, I discovered a glimmer of hope. Drawing upon my own experiences of struggle and despair, I once again found solace in writing—a cathartic outlet for my pain and a beacon of light in the darkness. It was during this time of crisis that I began to see (and research) the power of storytelling, recognizing that my words had the potential to heal and inspire first myself and then others who were struggling with their own challenges and demons.

With newfound clarity and purpose, I embarked on a journey of self-discovery and reinvention. I began to work on healing from trauma through counseling therapy, solid and uplifting relationships, and much more. I also sought out training in mental health and suicide prevention, determined to use my voice to make a difference in the lives of others. As I shared my story with audiences across the country, I realized that my calling extended far beyond the confines of the stage—I was meant to be an agent of hope for those who had temporarily lost their way.

In 2012, on the eve of my 28th birthday, I made a bold decision to take control of my destiny. I embraced a new chapter as a full-time speaker and writer. It was a leap of faith—moving away from the (semi) consistency of acting and bartending—that would test my limits and push me to new heights of success.

Yet, with success came its own set of challenges. As the demands of my work grew—more than 40 speaking events per year, along with all the administrative work and tasks associated with running a business—I found myself struggling to strike a balance between ambition and self-care. The temptation to take on too much was ever-present, threatening to overwhelm me with endless tasks and responsibilities.

But through it all, I remained steadfast in my commitment to growth and learning. I learned the importance of delegation, of trusting others to share the burden of responsibility. I discovered the power of cultivating meaningful relationships in all aspects of life (business, family, friendships, and more), recognizing that success is not measured by individual achievements, but by the strength of the bonds we forge with others.

Above all, I learned to prioritize my own well-being, recognizing that true success begins with self-care. In a world that often glorifies hustle and grind, I discovered the profound but simple truth that our greatest asset is not our productivity, but our humanity. I and we are valuable for simply showing up, for "being." And in embracing this truth, I found the freedom to live authentically and unapologetically.

As I reflect on the journey that has brought me to this moment, I am filled with gratitude for the lessons learned and the challenges I've overcome. From New York and regional theatrical stages to running a business, I have weathered the storms of adversity and emerged stronger, wiser, and more resilient than ever before.

And so, to anyone who dares to chase their dreams: Take care of yourself, first and foremost. Success is not a destination, but a journey—a journey that requires patience, perseverance, and above all, self-compassion. The true measure of success lies not in what we achieve, but in the lives, we touch and the hearts we inspire along the way.

HEIKE JOST, MFA

CEO AND CO-FOUNDER AT VOIGTMANN INC (HEALTH/MEDTECH) & EXECUTIVE DIRECTOR OF ARTFROG ART ACADEMY

Heike Jost has been helping businesses and individuals grow since 1996, offering guidance and advice in both personal and professional development globally, in both the United States and Europe, particularly for startups and entrepreneurs. She also offered website solutions tailored for the visually impaired and IT products designed for diverse user personas. Alongside her consulting and coaching work, she's launched multiple ventures spanning art, education, healthcare, IT, food technology, and more. Known for her design, creative, and innovative thinking, relentless learning, and ability to connect the dots, she excels at crafting holistic solutions that are both authentic and sustainable.

Methodology

Jost advises novice consultants to prioritize finding optimal solutions for businesses. She emphasizes the importance of adopting a mindset that involves innovating from scratch, picking up where others left off, and continuously refining your approach to align with your plan and budget. By blending a strong work ethic, perseverance, and determination with agile and creative thinking on a global scale, she aims to deliver smarter products and a brighter future for her clients.

Takeaways

- Try to explore innovative solutions tailored to the client's unique needs and challenges.
- Learn how to boost the client's business profitability and streamline development processes.
- Gain insights into branding and marketing strategies that set you apart from the competition.
- Tap into becoming an expert in regulatory environments, UN Sustainable Development Projects, and ethical AI practices.
- Have a mindset of building a stronger community and brand identity.
- Practice the process of solutions customization to meet the specific needs of your target audience.
- Only commit to tasks or actions that you'd be comfortable doing again.
- Avoid offering advice to individuals you don't get along with.
- Analyze thoroughly both what you consult for and your competitors.
- Ensure your brain and body are adequately rested for optimal performance.
- Practice active listening, increase your reading, and acknowledge achievements.

Hanane Anoua

Leadership and Mindset Coach, Facilitator, Keynote Speaker, and Author of Be Your Best

In 2016, I found myself abruptly displaced from my role as a regional marketing manager, along with other board members, due to a company restructuring. This happened one week after my dad passed away, which made it even harder for me.

During my new quest for new employment, I encountered multiple rejections. One day, I received an email from a press company, with whom I had multiple interviews, confirming that I was a great fit for the company. It was a big relief for me. It gave me hope again. Yet, this optimism was short-lived as a subsequent email dashed my hopes, citing a preference for a native English writer.

My disappointment was so great that I decided to start writing on social media to try to alleviate my pain. To my surprise, these writings brought significant engagement, and great positive feedback from my network. Continuously writing on social media not only inspired many but also helped me navigate through adversity.

In writing these motivational posts every day, I was also motivating myself to never give up. In inspiring people to believe in themselves, I was discovering more about myself. In empowering others, I was overcoming my own frustrations and anger. In spreading optimism and positive energy, I was growing more positive and resilient.

I did not know that my words would travel the world, resonate with many people, and touch the hearts of millions. This experience made me feel stronger and more positive about creating a new vision for myself.

Reinventing Myself

I decided to quit the corporate world and started from scratch in my new career in coaching and empowerment. I did not have all the skills and the competencies to perform at my best in the beginning. I started with fears and doubt, and I did not have all the steps in my mind, but my mind was my best asset that helped me make things happen.

Deciding to follow my passion caused me to lose a lot of people, but along the way, I gained many friends and mentors who believed in me and supported me to make my vision a reality.

In 2017, I started teaching soft skills to undergraduate and graduate students in national and international universities. In 2018, I became part of the board of coaches for designing and implementing the first soft skills curricular programs for Moroccan public universities.

In the same year, I joined an international foundation as a senior expert in women's empowerment to raise women's participation in politics in Morocco and Benin. I had the chance to train and empower women activists, heads of political parties, members of parliament, thought leaders, and entrepreneurs.

In 2021, I moved from Casablanca to Seattle, embarking on another chapter of reinvention. This transition, though daunting, reinforced the invaluable lesson of embracing change and stepping out of my comfort zone. Taking risks and trying new things started to become part of who I am.

Key Lessons Learned

The journey to success can be filled with uncertainty and challenges; it requires patience and a lot of persistence. What is truly beautiful about it is that, in the end, your success isn't just measured by the number of achievements you accomplished but by the person you've become along the way, something that no one can take from you.

Embrace rejections as redirections, failures as seeds of growth, and challenges as puzzles to put together to guide you to find a sense of meaning and create a new vision for yourself. Trust in your journey no matter what happens, even in the absence of the results you desire. Believe that you will get what you need at the right moment, not when you want it to happen.

Operating from stress, anxiety, or a low level of energy will attract the same level of energy manifested through detours, deceptions, or loss of opportunities. Surrounding yourself with people who uplift you and support you, like friends and mentors, fosters a positive environment for pursuing ambitious goals and effecting positive change.

Above all, be grateful as you will realize the blessings of those rejections months or years later. I am thankful to those who rejected me as I would not be here.

Riz Majumder

Management Consultant, Aspiring Author and Speaker

In the world of career choices, I found myself at a crossroads, pondering the many roads that lay ahead. The conventional route of a nine-to-five job promised stability and routine. The less-trodden path of consultancy held the attraction of independence, adventure, and innovation.

The Evolution
My journey toward becoming a consultant was not a sudden leap but rather a gradual evolution. I had worked at two Fortune 500 companies in managerial capacities, as a CEO of a software start-up, explored entrepreneurship, and even worked in management at a public sector organization.

I learned over the span of my professional career that I enjoyed growing and building a company/organization that deeply understands its business, the needs of its customers, and the broader marketplace in which it operates.

The Leap
I had just left a very stressful workplace. My finances were not in the best of shape, and I was dealing with issues in my personal life. I was very apprehensive about getting another conventional nine-to-five job. My inner voice was speaking to me about unfulfilled potential and unrealized dreams.

I knew that I had a proven track record of producing consistent double-digit gains in profitability for a wide variety of enterprises as manager, project manager, and senior executive.

It was then that I made the audacious decision to tread the path less traveled—to become an independent consultant.

What I Have Gained
Consultancy has offered me the freedom to design my own schedule, to travel, and to make connections beyond geographical and

organizational boundaries. It has granted me the autonomy to harness my creativity, challenge conventional wisdom, and redefine the concept of what is possible.

For me, consultancy is a calling that allows me to innovate, foster collaboration, and make a difference in the personal and professional lives of people and organizations.

Iwona Wilson

Certified International Facilitator, Author, Speaker, Coach, And Founder/CEO wilson.biz

I grew up in Poland in a family full of entrepreneurs. Back then, everyone was starting their own business because the country had just become a democracy. So, business talk was all around me as a kid.

My dad had a construction company, and my mom ran her clothes shop. Business talk was the norm at home, but honestly, I wasn't too keen on joining the family trend.

I remember my parents were always working, barely taking a break. Seeing that made me think twice about following in their footsteps. What I really wanted was to travel, meet new people, and enjoy long vacations, not be tied down to work all the time.

I started off in the U.K., working in the oil and gas business. Then I moved to Australia and got into project facilitation, which I loved. Eventually, I ended up in the U.S., starting my own consulting company. It's been a wild ride, full of unexpected twists, but my passion for helping people and facing challenges head-on made it all happen.

The Corporate Journey Begins

My early career kicked off in the U.K., where I worked as a Quality Assurance Manager on complex projects. It was here I had a major realization: to solve problems effectively, those impacted by these issues need to be part of finding the solution. This insight was a turning point, shaping my approach to work and collaboration.

Then, something unexpected happened. I was headhunted by Australia's largest energy producer. They didn't just hire me; they trained me to be a facilitator and project governance expert. It was an incredible opportunity, and I totally loved it. In Australia, I wasn't just doing a job; I was learning valuable tools that could make a real difference in how groups made decisions.

Life in Australia was amazing. I was deep into my role, using my skills to help teams work better together. The job was rewarding, and I was soaking up every minute of it. I loved my life so much that the thought of working on my own never crossed my mind. Being part of a high-profile company had its perks. I was surrounded by smart, ambitious people, the work was diverse, and the financial security was comforting. It seemed like the perfect setup to just settle down and focus on family and raising kids.

But, as I like to think of it, God had different plans for me. My journey was about to take another twist, leading me down a path I hadn't anticipated. It was this blend of real-world problem-solving in the U.K. and the advanced training in Australia that prepared me for what was to come, setting the stage for a shift from the corporate world to entrepreneurship.

The American Transition and COVID-19

The next chapter of my life began when my husband landed an exciting contract in South Texas. With our daughter being three years old and our son just 18 months, and my corporate life already scaled down to part-time, the timing felt right. We saw it as an adventure, planning to spend a few years in the USA before heading back home.

But then, just before COVID hit, life in the USA turned out to be incredibly tough. Beyond the typical challenges of moving to a new country, I faced a personal crisis. I struggled with my identity. My life had flipped upside down – no job, no friends, and no sense of home. For the first time, I realized how much of my identity was tied to being a working professional. Without my career, I felt lost, questioning who I was and what my purpose was.

On the other hand, the pandemic, while harrowing, brought clarity to my values, with love and freedom emerging as guiding lights. The absence of familiar professional opportunities forced me to consider entrepreneurship—a path I had never envisioned for myself.

The Birth of a Consulting Firm

Starting my own business wasn't really what I wanted, but I didn't have much choice. Jobs were hard to find, and I wanted to help people sort out their problems and make good decisions. So, I decided to set up my own consulting firm. It was tough in the beginning – I had to get an office ready, create a website, and go all out on marketing and social media. Plus, moving from Australia to South Texas was a huge change. I missed how things were and felt pretty alone, which made getting started even harder.

The other thing is that having my own business forced me to rethink everything about myself – my beliefs, actions, and ways of being. I had to create a new vision for myself, one that aligned with my current reality and aspirations.

Breakthrough and Expansion

Things started looking up about a year after I kicked off my business. I began connecting more with the folks around me, which helped. Landing my first client was a big deal—it wasn't just good for my business, but it also felt like I had finally overcome the struggles of moving to a new place and getting used to a different culture.

Then, life threw us another curveball. We moved again, this time to a small city in Southwest Florida.

Starting over in a new place meant I had to face a whole set of challenges to get my business up and running again.

Growing Roots in Florida

It was in Florida that my business truly began to flourish. The state's vibrant atmosphere and the warm, welcoming community played a pivotal role in the growth of my consulting firm. I tapped into an incredible network of CEOs, business founders, and academia, each connection opening new doors and opportunities. The real breakthrough came with the launch of the Sunshine Summit. This event allowed me to showcase my facilitation skills and share my passion for helping groups make better decisions and work more effectively together.

In Florida, I refined my offerings, packaging my services in a way that resonated with both local and international companies. This strategic approach not only clarified my value proposition but also made it easier for clients to understand and engage with my business. Reflecting on my journey, I've gleaned some invaluable insights:

Know Yourself and Your Purpose

Remembering who you are and what you're here to achieve is key. That's why it's important for folks to get into personal and professional development programs. These can help you figure out what you need and want in life.

Package Your Knowledge Well

Explaining what you're good at in a clear and catchy way is super important. It makes selling and marketing a whole lot easier and helps clients get what you're offering. It took me a while to get this. Moving from being an in-house facilitator to working independently meant I had to figure out how to show businesses and owners why I was valuable. By putting my skills into neat packages, I learned how to tweak my services to suit different clients better.

Focus on What Works

A single, effective funnel can be more valuable than multiple average ones. Pay attention to where your income originates and prioritize investing in those areas. Less is often more when it comes to resource allocation and strategic focus.

Wrap Up

My consulting firm's journey is more than just starting a business. It shows how important it is to be resilient, adaptable, and open to change. Every step, from my corporate days in the U.K. and Australia to starting my own business in the US, has helped me build a company that doesn't just survive tough times but truly succeeds. It's a story that might inspire anyone thinking about the big leap into starting their own business. And guess what? This is just the beginning; I'm only getting started.

DR. AHMED ZOUHAIR - CONSULTING, SPEAKER, AUTHOR

After graduating from college, most of my classmates had already secured positions with major petroleum companies, while I found myself on a six-month job hunt. My first role was far from glamorous – as an offshore mud sample catcher. I earned a modest $25 per day, enduring 12-hour shifts on oil and gas rigs, collecting mud every two hours. This opportunity came about through a response to an employment ad in the Houston Chronicle newspaper, with the mud logging company founded by CEO and President Mr. George Drewery. My subsequent role as a Measurement While Drilling (MWD) service petroleum engineer with Schlumberger provided invaluable lessons in resilience and adaptability. Working in such demanding conditions alongside esteemed mentors, I absorbed crucial skills in patience, active listening, and effective problem-solving. The constant client interactions at the rig site further helped accelerate my abilities and capabilities, ultimately laying the groundwork for my future success as an independent consultant.

For me, the journey to entrepreneurship was a testament to perseverance and continuous growth.

My Philosophy

I strongly believe in cultivating a broad perspective in all aspects of life, firmly trusting that it fosters open-mindedness and paves the way for boundless opportunities. This philosophy extends beyond my individual growth; it resonates deeply with how I approach business leadership. By embracing diversity of thought and fostering an inclusive environment, it has helped me unlock pathways to enhanced growth, continuous improvement, and sustainable success.

Moreover, I believe that the transformative power of connections is formed through openness and collaboration. By building bridges across industries and cultures, I have been able to cultivate networks that fuel growth and drive positive change on a global scale. In essence, I believe that the value of a wide perspective underscores the profound impact that open-minded leadership can have on individuals, organizations, and society as a whole.

My Purpose

I strongly desire to inspire and empower individuals to reach their fullest potential. Driven by a passion for continual learning, I have discovered my IKIGAI—a purpose rooted in speaking, coaching, business consulting, mentoring, and facilitating the success of professionals and entrepreneurs in their chosen endeavors. My mission is to serve as a catalyst for growth and fulfillment, guiding others toward realizing their aspirations and achieving excellence in all facets of their lives.

My guiding principles (a.k.a. my core values) are to be compassionate, cooperative, collaborative, trustworthy, and honest with my clients and teams.

Key Concepts Learned from My Consulting Journey

- Transitioning from a salaried, full-time job to independent consulting provided me with more freedom in both work and life.

- Consultants often earn a better wage than salaried employees because of their expertise.
- There are numerous opportunities to improve your personal and professional development.
- Consulting may be difficult at first, but once you find your ideal client or clients, you will likely be set for life.
- Companies are always looking for outside resources because of the development of new ideas, new governmental relations, and internal and external growth. Generally, as a consultant, you don't have to deal with internal bureaucracy.
- Major big consulting firms are known for non-ethical practices for winning major contracts because of their political involvement in lobbying. To compensate for this, major government entities are required to give opportunities to small, minority independent contractors and have created hubs for them.
- There are accounting and financial incentives for independent consultants (consult an accountant and/or a financial advisor to learn more)

Essential Takeaways to Have Success as a Consultant

Pursuing a career in consulting necessitates developing critical abilities, strategic planning, and a broad awareness of the field. A crucial part of marketing, branding, and improving online presence is offering a great consulting service to clients. Consulting today covers a wide range of services. Understanding the complexities of the consulting landscape—from terminology and client relationships to the tools and procedures that support efficient consulting—is essential for navigating this fast-paced industry.

Effective communication, the capacity to solve problems, and flexibility become essential qualities in the consulting process. A comprehensive approach to skill development is essential, encompassing everything from problem-solving and issue identification to acquiring technical, experience, and people skills. The path to becoming a consultant entails pursuing a professional path that calls for self-analysis, competence evaluation, and the deliberate identification of consulting services requirements.

When one explores the complexities of project management, they learn the value of efficient preparation, communication, and flexibility. Consultants may effectively manage varied projects by utilizing proactive problem-solving techniques, strategic decision-making, and continual improvement. Niche consulting offers advantages, including improved credibility, increased profitability, and more effective marketing campaigns. In order to become an authority in a certain field, one must carefully investigate, network, learn continuously, and communicate well in order to cultivate a niche.

All things considered, consulting is a dynamic and diverse field that requires a mix of technical expertise, strategic thought, and good communication. To succeed in this sector, one must be flexible, dedicated to lifelong learning, and have a solid professional network. consultants may succeed in their careers and make a significant impact on the businesses and industry at large by learning the ins and outs of the consulting environment, honing critical skills, utilizing tools skillfully, and providing real value.

CHAPTER 11

FINAL THOUGHTS

When independent consulting is your business, you become the product and the service you provide for the business. As you develop your consulting business, remember to engage in a healthy work-life balance—many consultants do not, and it is detrimental to their health as well as their personal and professional relationships.

Your client's demands may be great, and the competition to gain business may be fierce, but you must take care of yourself and spend quality time with your friends and family, take care of your health, exercise, eat nourishing foods, smile, have fun, and avoid burnout, stress, and depression.

Companies hire consultants or contractors because they get the job done no matter what, and also because they are relatively faster, better, cheaper (no provided benefits such as healthcare), and much more. So, start putting your plan together to become an independent consultant.

I have some good news for you—your career as a successful independent consultant is within reach. All you have to do is take the first step to make it a reality. Come back to this book and use it as a guide or roadmap to help you make continual progress.

As you embark upon your journey to become an independent consultant, you can reach out to me or any of the consultants who contributed to this book for guidance, services, mentoring, or coaching.

If this book has helped you in any way, please leave an honest review online. By doing so, you will ensure that others who need this book will be able to organically discover this book and utilize its lessons.

Congratulations on your future success! I can't wait to hear all about it!

- Ahmed Zouhair

ACKNOWLEDGMENTS

Special thanks to all who volunteered to write their case studies and share their experience with you: Trevor Perry, Yassine Touimi Benjelloun, Josh Rivedal, Heike Jost, Hanane Anoua, Riz Majumder, and Iwona Wilson.

Thanks to you for reading this book. Now it's your turn to get out and start hustling and consulting. It will change your life forever!

ABOUT THE AUTHOR

Ahmed Zouhair, DBA, PMP

Fluent in three languages (Arabic, French, and English) and with three degrees—including a doctorate in Business Administration—serial entrepreneur and seasoned project, product, and program management consultant Ahmed Zouhair knows the value of hard work. He also understands what it takes to build an empire from scratch. While today his international roster of clients includes companies and individuals from the education, IT, telecommunications, digital security, oil and gas, finance and banking, and non-profit sectors, Ahmed's career didn't start out that way. His first job after college involved collecting mud samples during 12-hour shifts on an oil and gas rig. Such tedious work in a harsh environment taught him patience and how to think on his feet when things go wrong. He likewise learned to interact with many different types of people, skills he would later refine as a volunteer business coach and workshop presenter for SCORE.

To hire Ahmed Zouhair to speak and or to do a workshop for your organization, visit theazinstitute.com or ahmedzouhair.com.

Reach out to Ahmed with any questions at azouhair2007@gmail.com or connect with him on LinkedIn.

OTHER WORKS

Demystifying Project Management: A Project Management Guide in Plain English for Startups

This book was deliberately written in straightforward, jargon-free language understandable by anyone with even a modest background in business. I designed it to show you how to manage projects of all types, small or large, local or global, in-person or digital, for any kind of organization. I want it to be your toolbox—and I'm looking at you, engineers, software developers, managers, and teachers. Your toolbox is what you go to without thinking, knowing it has everything you need.

My hope is that it will lend structure to concepts you already know, show you how to apply those concepts properly, and serve as an ongoing reference book any time you're managing a project.

Demystifying Career Paths: The Essential Guide to Job-Seeking

This book outlines the step-by-step process of finding a job, challenging readers to think critically about their careers. Inside, author Ahmed Zouhair talks about creating a job search "roadmap" that will help professionals land their dream job. This book also covers how to manage one's career as a mini project using the 4P's—Perspective, Preparation, Plan, Performance—and with tools, tips, and techniques to create a meaningful and impactful career path.

Demystifying Network Paths: Network for New Worth, Finding Authentic and Meaningful Connections

Demystifying Networking Paths offers new ways to nurture and grow your network by building relationships based on trust and empathy, showing that you can add value to others and benefit from the power of networking by simply changing perspectives about networking. If you're looking to change how you network or simply need to step up your networking game, then you need to pick up a copy of this book!

www.ingramcontent.com/pod-product-compliance
Lightning Source LLC
Chambersburg PA
CBHW030447220526
45464CB00006B/2441